Life in the
THIRTEEN COLONIES

Virginia

Sandra Pobst

children's press®
An imprint of
SCHOLASTIC

Library of Congress Cataloging-in-Publication Data

Pobst, Sandra.
  Virginia / by Sandra Pobst.
    p. cm. — (Life in the thirteen colonies)
  Includes bibliographical references and index.
  ISBN 0-516-24580-5
  1. Virginia—History—Colonial period, ca. 1600-1775—Juvenile literature.
  2. Virginia—History—1775-1865—Juvenile literature. I. Title. II. Series.
  F229.P78 2004
  975.5'02—dc22

                              2004010126

A Creative Media Applications Production
Design: Fabia Wargin Design
Production: Alan Barnett, Inc.
Editor: Matt Levine
Copy Editor: Laurie Lieb
Proofreader: Betty Pessagno
Content Research: Lauren Thogersen
Photo Researcher: Annette Cyr
Content Consultant: David Silverman, Ph.D.

CONTENTS

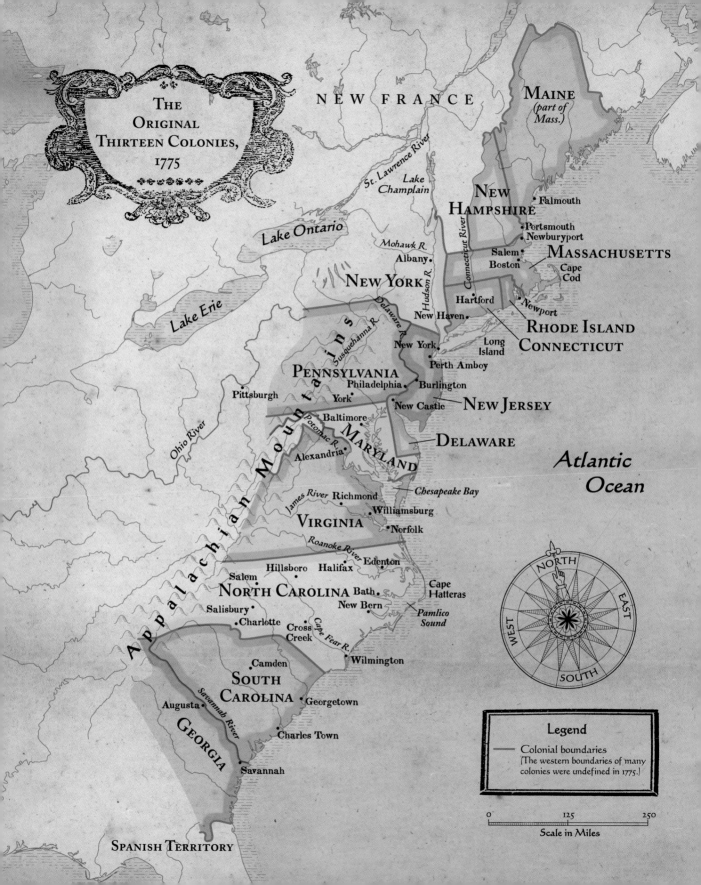

A Nation Grows
From Thirteen Colonies

Virginia is located in the southeastern part of the United States. It is bordered by Maryland, West Virginia, Kentucky, North Carolina, and Tennessee. Chesapeake Bay and the Atlantic Ocean make up part of its eastern border as well.

The colony began with the settlement of Jamestown, the first permanent English town in America. The region was home to many Native American tribes. They lived along Virginia's shores and throughout its forested hills and mountains.

Virginia was a leader in the fight for freedom from England. Many future U.S. presidents were from Virginia. George Washington and Thomas Jefferson were among the most important people in colonial America.

The map shows the thirteen English colonies in 1775. The colored sections show the areas that were settled at that time.

CHAPTER ONE

The English Arrive

A New Venture

Queen Elizabeth I listened intently as Walter Raleigh tried to convince her to establish colonies in the New World. (Europeans considered Europe the Old World. They called North and South America the New World.) Raleigh pointed out that gold, silver, and other treasures from Spanish colonies had enriched Spain's treasury for nearly a hundred years. An English colony in North America could do the same for England.

Spain was one of England's greatest rivals. Raleigh noted that an English colony could be used as a base from which to attack the Spanish colonies. This would help

Sir Walter Raleigh was an explorer and adventurer. He sailed to America in 1578 and decided it was the perfect place for an English colony.

England control Spain's growing power. Colonizing America could also solve the problem of the growing number of unemployed people in England. People without jobs could be sent to America to work for England.

Convinced by Raleigh's arguments, Queen Elizabeth granted him the right to colonize America. In 1584, Raleigh organized an **expedition**, led by Philip Amadas and Arthur Barlowe. Their mission was to sail to America and locate a good site for England's first colony.

Amadas and his men arrived off the coast of North America in the summer of 1584. Their voyage from

John White, one of the first English colonists, drew pictures of the Roanoke Island Indians fishing from dugout canoes.

England had taken three months. The crew anchored the ships, and a small group of men rowed to the sandy beach. With great pride, they claimed the entire Atlantic coast of North America "in the name of God and Queen Elizabeth."

As the men explored, they realized they were on an island that ran alongside the mainland. This barrier island protected the mainland from high tides and stormy seas. The island was called Roanoke. From the western shore, the men could see the woodlands of the mainland. Large flocks of birds lived on the island, and grapes grew everywhere.

The Native Virginians

The English explorers ignored the fact that Woodland Indian tribes had lived in the region for centuries. The English believed that their way of life was far superior to that of the "savages" who lived in America. They were sure that the Indians would welcome them and willingly adopt English customs.

The first English explorers were right about one thing. The Native Americans who lived nearby *did* welcome them. The Roanoke Island Indians were used to trading with strangers from other tribes. They soon arrived to trade and invited Barlowe and seven others to visit their village.

Roanoke

Wingina, chief of the Roanoke Island Indians, welcomed the explorers warmly. Since it was summer when Barlowe and his men arrived on Roanoke Island, food was plentiful. Wingina fed the visitors as a gesture of friendship and respect. Little did he realize that future English settlers would expect his tribe to supply their food as well.

Wingina's village was built in a style similar to those of other Algonquian tribes living along the mid-Atlantic coast. (The Algonquian were a group of Indian tribes with similar languages and customs.) A wall made of sharpened stakes, called a **palisade**, surrounded the village. This wall provided protection from enemy attacks. Inside the palisade were longhouses made from saplings (young trees) that were bent and tied together at the top. The bent trees formed a series of arches. These tunnel-shaped homes were covered with mats woven from reeds or bark. These mats could be raised or lowered to let light in and smoke out. A door was placed at one end of the longhouse, and fires were built in the center.

The Algonquian tribes hunted, fished, and farmed. The men were skilled hunters, and meals typically included meat from animals such as deer and turkeys. Fish were also plentiful. The main crop of the Algonquin was corn. They also grew squash, pumpkins, and beans. They raised enough corn so that some could be stored and eaten in the winter. Often, however, all the stored corn would be eaten before the new crop was harvested. Hunger was common at the end of the winter and during the spring months.

Roanoke Island Indians were very interested in the English explorers. But they also found the Europeans frightening. After all, the strange men carried weapons that shot fire (muskets) and English armor looked like metal skin.

Most terrifying of all was the effect of European diseases on the Native American population. Barlowe and his crew helped introduce smallpox, measles, and other diseases to America. The Native Americans had no natural protection against these diseases. Thousands of Indians became infected and died. The Indians did not understand why they often became sick and died soon after meeting the newcomers. Many Indians believed that the white men were killing them with their thoughts. Several years later, in 1590, Thomas Harriot wrote about this in a book about his trip to Roanoke:

> within a few dayes after our departure from
> everie such towne, the people began to die very fast,
> and many in short space; ... They were perswaded
> [persuaded] that it was the worke of our God
> through our meanes, and that wee by him might
> kil and slai [slay] whom wee would without
> weapons and not come neere them.

Reaction to the Expedition

When the explorers returned to England later that year, Barlowe described all the wonderful things he had discovered on Roanoke Island. He noted that it was "a most pleasant and fertile ground, replenished with goodly Cedars, and divers other sweete woods, full of Corrants [grapes], flaxe, and many other notable commodities [valuable products]." He also reported that the Indians in the region were "gentle, loving, and faithfull." As proof, the expedition brought two Algonquian Indians with them to England. Manteo and Wanchese were chiefs of the Croatoan and Roanoke Island tribes. The two returned to America in 1585.

Queen Elizabeth was delighted with the success of the expedition. She rewarded Raleigh by making him an English **knight**. Almost immediately, Raleigh began making plans for a permanent colony on Roanoke Island. He named the new land Virginia in honor of Queen Elizabeth. (Elizabeth was known as the Virgin Queen, since she had never married.)

Roanoke Island would one day become part of the colony of North Carolina. It was included in the land that Queen Elizabeth gave to Raleigh to start the new colony called Virginia.

Roanoke Colony

In 1585, Raleigh sent seven ships to Roanoke Island to establish a military colony. Sir Richard Grenville, one of England's most admired naval officers, was in command of the fleet. More than 500 men were aboard. The ships reached the islands south of Roanoke Island in late June. The crews spent a month exploring the coastal region as they made their way to Roanoke.

As the fleet neared Roanoke Island, several ships struck rocks in shallow water and sank. The supplies needed to get the colony off to a strong start were ruined. As a result, Grenville did not stay long on Roanoke Island. Instead, he sailed back to England to get new supplies. The colonists and soldiers were left under the command of Ralph Lane. Lane became the acting governor of Roanoke Colony.

Among this first group of colonists were brick makers, carpenters, and thatchers (people who made roofs from reeds or straw). There were also many soldiers who had experience building forts. These skills were put to use right away. The colonists set to

Unlimited Land

Since America was largely unexplored by the English at the time Roanoke was settled, the boundaries of the new land were vague. At one time, Virginia Colony included all or part of present-day Illinois, Indiana, Kentucky, Michigan, Minnesota, North Carolina, Ohio, Virginia, West Virginia, and Wisconsin.

work building an earthen fort with a star-shaped outer wall. Known as Fort Raleigh, it was too small for any houses to be built inside the walls. The men built their houses outside the fort. These houses were similar to those found in England at the time, with thatched roofs and brick chimneys.

Although winter was not far off, the colonists did not try to plant any crops. Few of the colonists had experience hunting animals for food. They simply assumed that the Indians in the area would supply their food. Governor Lane persuaded Wingina to plant extra corn both on the island and the mainland. The Roanoke Island tribe also set up wooden fences called weirs to trap fish for the colonists.

While the Indians were busy growing extra food, the colonists set off to explore their new territory. Groups traveled about 80 miles (128 kilometers) south of Roanoke Island and as far north as Chesapeake Bay. Taking part in the expedition was scientist Thomas Harriot. Harriot made detailed descriptions of the plant and animal life found in Virginia. These were later published in the book *A Briefe and True Report of the New Found Land of Virginia*. John White, an artist in the group, sketched the plant and animal life in the area and the Indians who lived there. His drawings were included in Harriot's book. The book captured the imagination of the English people and made them very interested in America.

Winter Hardships

As winter chilled the air, the colonists returned to Fort Raleigh. When their supplies ran low, they demanded that Wingina give them corn and other food. At first, Wingina was willing to share the tribe's food with the colonists. But when the English demanded more, the Indians grew angry and resentful. If they continued to give food to the colonists, their own families would go hungry. Wingina finally refused to give the colonists any more food.

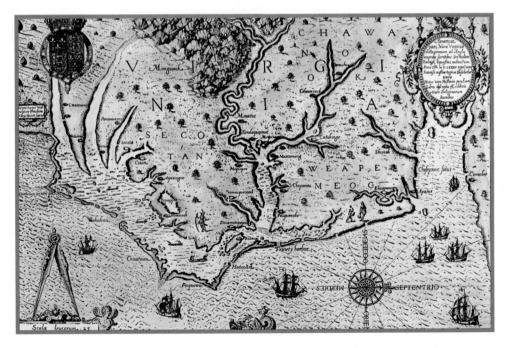

Thomas Harriot and John White explored the territory around Roanoke and made detailed maps of the Virginia colony.

The colonists and Roanoke Island Indians fought with each other and destroyed villages and crops.

The Indians and colonists quarreled over food and the right to hunting grounds. Governor Lane believed that the Indians planned to attack Fort Raleigh. He decided to strike first. Lane gathered his soldiers and led an attack on the Indian village. The English settlers killed Wingina.

The Indians fought back against the settlers. They destroyed the weirs they had built for the colonists. In return, the settlers burned the Indians' cornfields. The situation quickly became desperate for the English. They had little food and almost no way to get more. In addition, they were constantly threatened by the Roanoke Indians.

Facing starvation, Governor Lane sent groups of ten to twenty men to live for a few weeks at a time on the other barrier islands. There, they could find oysters and mussels to eat while they watched for ships that might take them back to England.

Those who stayed at Fort Raleigh continued their war against Wingina's people. Many were killed on both sides. The Indians who had welcomed the English to Roanoke Island were now their bitter enemies.

Rescue

On June 9, 1586, the weary colonists received exciting news from those who had been sent to the other islands. Sir Francis Drake and his fleet of twenty-three ships were within a day's voyage of the colony. Drake was an English sea captain sent on a voyage of discovery by Queen Elizabeth.

When Drake arrived, he found Roanoke Colony in shambles. The captain offered the colonists two choices. He could provide enough supplies to last a month and leave one of his ships in case they decided to return to England later. Or the settlers could travel back to England with Drake immediately.

Governor Lane accepted the offer of supplies and a ship. But the ship was lost in a storm before they could get it ready to sail for England. Luckily, Drake had not yet left Roanoke with his fleet. Since Lane did not know when or if Grenville would return, he gave the order to abandon Fort Raleigh. He and the settlers returned to England with Drake's fleet.

Not long after the colonists left, a supply ship sent by Raleigh reached Roanoke. When no colonists could be found, the ship returned to England. A few weeks later, Grenville arrived on another ship. He found only empty buildings and the ruins of Fort Raleigh. Grenville set sail for home. But he left fifteen men on the island to protect England's claim to the colony.

The Second Colony

In spite of the failure of Roanoke Colony, Raleigh was determined to establish an English colony in Virginia. He organized another group of settlers in May 1587. This time, 150 people boarded ships to sail for America. Some of these colonists, including the new governor, John White, had been part of the first effort to settle Roanoke. Most of the colonists on this second voyage wanted the chance to live on land of their own. Most people in England did not have their own land. They rented land to farm from rich landowners. Raleigh promised the new settlers their own land if they moved to Virginia. This prospect was very appealing to poor farmers who wanted a better life for themselves and their families. This time, women and children were part of the group traveling to America.

Raleigh issued orders that the new colony should be established on the mainland in the Chesapeake Bay area, north of Roanoke. He probably wanted to avoid further fighting between the colonists and the Roanoke Island Indians. On the way to Chesapeake Bay, Governor White decided to stop at Roanoke Island. He wanted to check on the fifteen men that Grenville had left there to guard Fort Raleigh the previous year. When the colonists arrived, they found no sign of the men.

For some unknown reason, Governor White decided to stay on Roanoke Island rather than continue on to Chesapeake Bay. This decision would haunt him for the rest of his life.

The Roanoke Island Indians were furious at the arrival of more English settlers. They launched attacks on the colonists, killing one man soon after the English reached the island. Seeing that Roanoke was unsafe, White led his group to the nearby island of Croatoan. The settlers met with the friendly Croatoan Indians who lived there. During that visit, the Croatoans told White that the Roanoke Island tribe had killed the fifteen men that Grenville had left behind the previous year.

White decided to seek revenge on the Roanoke Island Indians. He led a group of men in an attack on their village and killed the Indians they found there. When the colonists investigated further, they found that the Indians they had killed were actually Croatoan, not Roanoke. The friendly Croatoan had been in the village looking for food. The Roanoke Island Indians had left the area before the attack.

The Lost Colony

White held to his decision to remain on Roanoke in spite of his troubles with the Indians. The newcomers began to build a settlement. Soon they were joined by a new colonist. White's daughter and her husband were among the settlers. On August 18, 1587, their daughter, Virginia Dare, was born in Roanoke Colony. Virginia was the first English child born in America. To the colonists, her birth was proof that Roanoke Colony would flourish and grow.

The English settlers had little time to celebrate. Cold weather would soon arrive, and they were not prepared. Little food had been stored for winter. The fighting with neighboring Indian tribes meant that the Indians would not share their food with the colonists. The only option was to sail to England for supplies.

Governor White agreed to make the long, dangerous trip. Everyone knew it could be six months or longer before White returned with supplies. The settlers came up with a plan for notifying White if they had to move from Roanoke Island.

When John White returned to Roanoke, he found the word CROATOAN carved into a tree trunk.

If the colonists had to leave, they would carve their destination into the trunk of a tree. If they were in danger when they left, they would also carve a cross in the tree trunk.

As it turned out, the timing of White's trip could not have been worse. England and Spain had been at war for nearly two years. While White was in England gathering supplies, the Spanish Armada, Spain's fleet of warships, attacked the country.

Mystery Solved?

Although no one knows what happened to the colonists left behind on Roanoke Island, there are many legends and theories. Some historians believe that the colonists made their way to a friendly Croatoan village and were adopted by the tribe. Others think the colonists moved north to Chesapeake Bay and were killed by tribes living in that region.

In 1719, hunters were traveling through a remote area of North Carolina about 100 miles (160 kilometers) from the original Roanoke settlement. They came across a group of light-skinned people with blue eyes living in the area. The people, known today as the Lumbee Indians, spoke the same style of English that was spoken in the late sixteenth century. They practiced the Christian religion and had the same last names as many of the Roanoke colonists, including Dare and White. Many people believe that the Lumbees are descendants of the Croatoan Indians and the people of the Lost Colony.

Queen Elizabeth commanded that all ships be placed in the service of the British navy to fight against the Spanish Armada. This included ships that were privately owned. White's ship was taken to help in the fight, so he could not leave the country. Although the Spanish Armada was defeated within a few months, naval battles raged in the Atlantic Ocean for the next few years. As a result, White was not able to return to America until 1590. This was three years after he had left Roanoke Island.

Finally, White sailed for America and arrived at Fort Raleigh. When he went ashore, he found no sign of the colonists. The houses had all been destroyed. Thick grass had overgrown what few English tools and objects remained. In place of the original earthen fort, a palisade surrounded the housing area. White searched for the signal the colonists had agreed to leave in case of emergency.

Soon he found a carving on one of the trees in the palisade. Cut into the tree trunk was the word "CROA-TOAN." There was no other carving and no cross to indicate the colonists had been in danger. White was certain that the colonists had traveled south to Croatoan Island. He guessed that they were seeking help from the Indians who had once befriended them.

White wanted to sail to Croatoan Island to look for his family and the other colonists. When he tried to make the journey, however, stormy weather made it too dangerous. Eventually, White gave up and sailed back to England. He never learned the fate of the colonists who had stayed at Roanoke. Today, the colony at Roanoke is known as the Lost Colony. Although many theories exist, no one has ever solved the mystery of its disappearance.

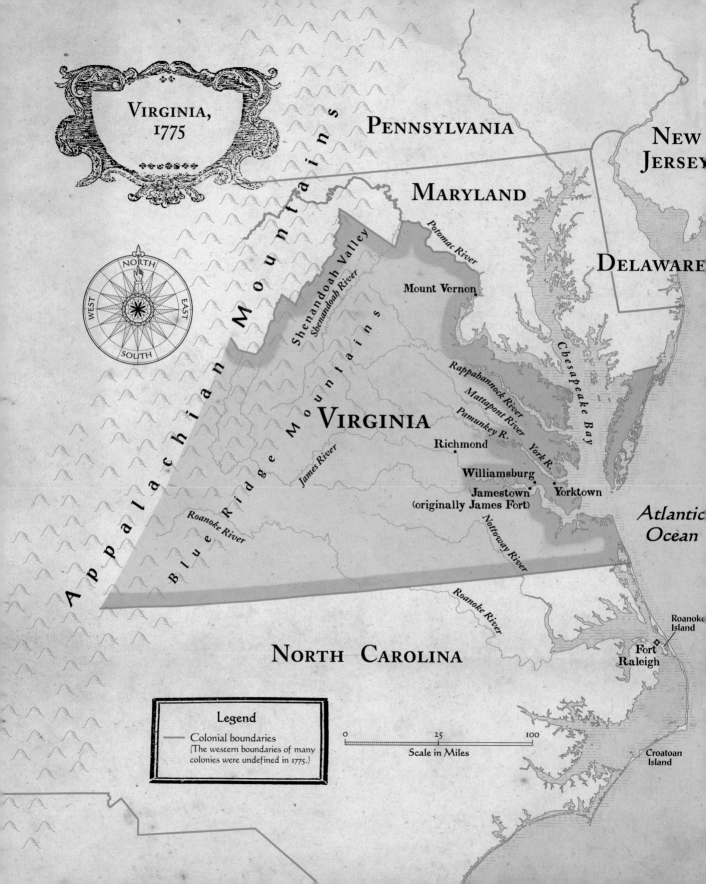

VIRGINIA, 1775

PENNSYLVANIA

NEW JERSEY

MARYLAND

DELAWARE

NORTH
WEST · EAST
SOUTH

Appalachian Mountains

Shenandoah Valley

Shenandoah River

Potomac River

Mount Vernon

Chesapeake Bay

Blue Ridge Mountains

VIRGINIA

Rappahannock River

Mattaponi River

Pamunkey R.

York R.

James River

Richmond

Williamsburg

Jamestown
(originally James Fort)

Yorktown

Atlantic Ocean

Roanoke River

Nottoway River

Roanoke River

NORTH CAROLINA

Roanoke Island

Fort Raleigh

Croatoan Island

Legend
Colonial boundaries
(The western boundaries of many colonies were undefined in 1775.)

0   25   100
Scale in Miles

CHAPTER TWO

A Permanent Settlement

After Roanoke Colony

By 1590, the English had failed twice to establish a colony in America. After the mysterious disappearance of the Lost Colony, many people in England did not want to send more settlers to America. More than a hundred English citizens had lost their lives in the colonies. Those who had invested in Roanoke Colony had lost great sums of money. Still, some Englishmen wanted to try again.

When Queen Elizabeth died in 1603, King James I became the new king of England. He was very interested in setting up colonies in America. He hoped the colonists would find gold in the New World. Also, people who imported goods from English colonies paid taxes to the English government.

⌦ *This map shows how Virginia looked in 1775.*

Establishing a new colony was expensive. Ships had to be bought to transport the settlers to America. The ships had to be filled with enough supplies to support the settlers, and soldiers had to be paid to protect them.

The king did not want to pay these expenses, so he encouraged a group of business leaders to form the Virginia Company. These people would pay to set up a new colony. In return, James gave a **charter** to the Virginia Company in 1606. The charter allowed the company to profit from any money the colony made. The charter also gave the company the power to appoint a governor and make the laws for the colony.

In order to get enough money to set up the colony, the business leaders sold shares in the company. This meant that anyone who paid a certain amount of money would be able to share in any profits the company made. Those who wanted to invest in the Virginia Company but did not want to move to America were called adventurers. Those who agreed to work for the company in the new colony were known as planters. Planters were not allowed to own land in America. All the land belonged to the Virginia Company. But the planters would share in any profits that the company made.

The Virginia Company set three main goals for the planters. First, they were to look for gold. Second, they were to try to discover a passage to China. And finally, they were to investigate all possible ways of making money in the New World.

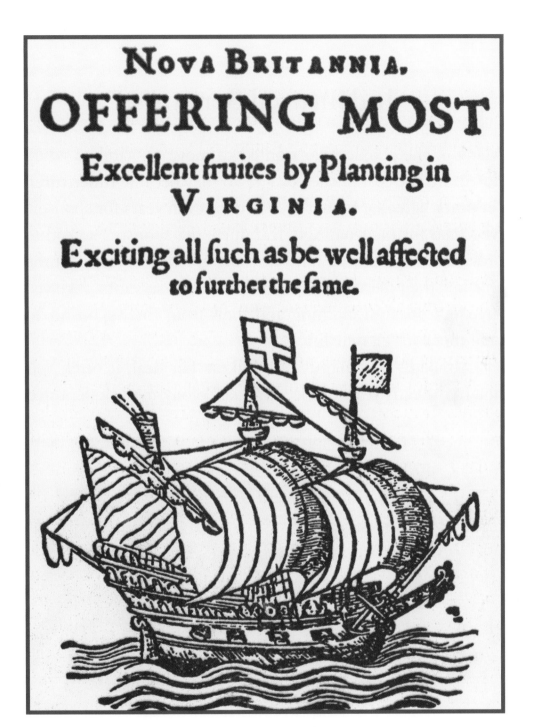

NOVA BRITANNIA,
OFFERING MOST
Excellent fruites by Planting in
VIRGINIA.

Exciting all such as be well affected
to further the same.

This pamphlet was published by the Virginia Company in 1609 to convince English people to move to Virginia.

Indentured Servants

Many of the people who wanted to move to Virginia could not afford the cost of the voyage. So they became **indentured servants**, agreeing to work for five to seven years for sponsors who paid for their passage. In return, the sponsors agreed to provide food, clothing, and housing for the servants. At the end of their service, many indentured servants received "freedom dues" of clothing and tools from their sponsors to help them start a new life.

Although this might sound like a fair deal, it often was not. In the early years of the Virginia Colony, many indentured

Many young men and women worked as indentured servants in places like this tavern to pay for their passage to Virginia.

servants worked for the Virginia Company. The servants were considered property, much like slaves, until their contracts were over. If the company needed more workers, it would just ignore the contract. People who had agreed to work five years often ended up being required to work ten or more years. Many indentured servants did not live long enough to gain the freedom for which they had worked so hard.

Not all indentured servants wanted to go to America. Some were kidnapped on the streets of England by ships' captains. They were then sold as indentured servants in America. Others were criminals who were given the choice between going to the colonies as indentured servants or going to prison.

Indentured servants made up the biggest group of **immigrants** to America in the early years of colonization. Some scholars estimate that between one-half and two-thirds of the settlers who arrived in America during the seventeenth century were indentured servants.

What's in a Name?

The people who agreed to work in return for a voyage to America became known as indentured servants because of the types of contracts they signed. After both parties signed the contract, the paper was torn in half. Each piece had a notch, or *indentation*, that the other piece fitted into like a puzzle piece. A master and servant each kept one half of the contract. When the contract was up, the two pieces were fitted together and the indentured servant became a free person.

The Journey Begins

By the end of 1606, the Virginia Company had three ships ready to sail for America—the *Susan Constant*, the *Godspeed*, and the *Discovery*. The expedition was under the leadership of Captain Christopher Newport. The 108 men and boys who boarded the ships were full of confidence. They expected to be in the New World in two months or so, starting the new colony and getting rich. Instead, winter

John White drew maps of Jamestown and the surrounding area.
These maps were used by colonists who followed the Lost Colony.

storms battered the boats. Winds kept blowing them back into the English Channel. Six weeks after they left for America, the settlers could still see England from the deck of the ship.

In addition to the usual supplies, maps, and orders, the Virginia Company gave Captain Newport a locked box. He was told to keep the box closed until the settlers arrived in Virginia. It contained the names of the men the Virginia Company had appointed to run the new colony.

Sailing to America

The ships that carried the colonists to America were nothing like today's large cruise ships. In fact, they were amazingly small. The *Susan Constant* was the largest of the ships that sailed on the 1606 voyage to America. It was just over 55 feet (16.5 kilometers) long and nearly 23 feet (7 meters) wide. Four ships would almost fit side-by-side on a high school basketball court.

The colonists, whether rich or poor, were given spaces below deck just big enough to stretch out in. Even less space was reserved for children. Here they remained for the entire voyage. In this dark, crowded space, there was little fresh air. Germs spread quickly, and many colonists got sick on the trip to America. Once the fresh food was gone, hard biscuits and moldy meat were often the only foods available.

The Colonists Arrive

In April 1607, after a journey of more than four months, 105 English colonists finally arrived in Chesapeake Bay. (Three men had died on the voyage.) With the ships anchored near the shore, a small group ventured out to explore the immediate area. They found both woods and meadows with many streams. As the colonists headed back to their boats, a group of Indians attacked them. The Englishmen fired their muskets at the Indians. This was the first of many hostile encounters with the Native Americans living near Chesapeake Bay.

The three boats remained at the mouth of Chesapeake Bay for a few weeks as the men explored the area. They feasted on wild strawberries and oysters that covered the ground "as thick as stones." Finally, the colonists gathered around Captain Newport as he opened the locked box that held their orders from the Virginia Company. The first thing he read was a list containing the names of the governing council that would oversee the new colony.

Everyone was shocked by one name on the list. It belonged to a man who had been arrested for **mutiny** during the long voyage. That man was Captain John Smith. Many of his fellow colonists found Smith annoying and disliked him. But it was Smith who would help the young colony survive its first few years.

Captain John Smith and the other colonists explored Chesapeake Bay using small boats.

New Leaders

After the governing council was identified, Newport read the orders from the Virginia Company. The colonists were to make their way up one of the rivers that drained into the bay. There, they were to locate an easily protected site for a fort. This location away from the bay would hide the new colony from Spanish ships that might sail by. Following these orders, the colonists sailed 60 miles (96 kilometers) up the southernmost river. They named it the James River in honor of the English king. In mid-May, they found a piece of land surrounded by deep water on three sides. They decided that this **peninsula** would be the perfect site for James Fort. The settlement would later become known as Jamestown.

As it turned out, the colonists had picked one of the worst spots possible for their settlement. The low-lying peninsula did not have a clean supply of drinking water. This lack of fresh water caused

The Jamestown colonists built log houses and surrounded them with a palisade after they were attacked by Indians.

The Anglican Church in Virginia

The Anglican Church (also known as the Church of England) was the official church in both England and the colony of Virginia. The king (or queen) of England was the head of the church. Anglican preachers were appointed by government leaders and required to swear loyalty to the king or queen. Their sermons were often intended to increase support for royal policies.

From the beginning, the Jamestown colonists were expected to follow strict laws established by the Anglican Church and the Virginia Company. They were required to attend church services twice daily, to observe the Sabbath (a holy day of rest), and to avoid immoral activities such as swearing or drinking heavily. Taxes collected from the colonists were used to support the church.

many deaths from a disease called dysentery. In the summer, swarms of mosquitoes blanketed the area. These mosquitoes carried malaria, another often fatal disease.

The colonists spent most of the first few days exploring the banks of the James River and looking for gold. Nobody showed much interest in starting construction on the fort. A few weeks after they arrived at James Fort, Indians attacked. Two of the colonists were killed and ten were wounded. After that, the men worked quickly to complete the triangular palisade that protected James Fort. Later, a storehouse, a church, and some houses would be built inside the palisade. With the fort in place, Captain Newport sailed back to England for supplies.

The First Jamestown Colonists

Packed among the supplies for Jamestown were tools for building houses and forts. However, the Virginia Company was so intent on finding gold and other treasures that it sent few farming tools. The company expected the colonists to get most of their food from the Indians. This foolish plan ignored the experiences of the Roanoke colonists two decades earlier. It created many hardships for the Jamestown colonists.

According to Captain John Smith's reports, more than half of the men who reached Jamestown in 1607 listed their occupation as "gentleman." The gentlemen were from wealthy families. Many had never worked for a living. They had packed up their best feathered hats, silk stockings, and wigs and sailed to America to find riches and adventure. Most of the men on the colony's governing council were gentlemen.

Six carpenters, one blacksmith, two bricklayers, and thirteen laborers were also in that first group of colonists. Their skills and strength would be in great demand during the hard work of building a colony. Many of the colonists' names did not appear on the list John Smith made of the first colonists. They were most likely indentured servants.

Four boys traveled to America in 1607. They were probably orphans or runaways who had been taken aboard ship as servants. Smith thought these boys could help the

John Smith

Without Captain John Smith's leadership, the second attempt to colonize Virginia might have failed like the first. Who was this brash, twenty-five-year-old who stepped aboard the *Susan Constant* in 1606, eager for new adventures in America?

As a young boy, John Smith longed to see the world. Orphaned at thirteen, Smith sold his schoolbooks and made plans to leave England. Three years later, he became a soldier for hire. Much later, Smith wrote of the glorious battles he had fought. During one fierce battle, Smith was captured and sold into slavery by the Turks. After a daring escape, he made his way back to England, fighting pirates and courting fair ladies along the way.

Finding England a little too tame, John Smith arranged with the Virginia Company to sail to America with the first group of colonists. The men he sailed with did not trust him. During the voyage, Smith was accused of plotting to take over the colony. Once in America, however, they were grateful for his skill in trading and his ability to establish relationships with the Indians.

colonists learn about the local Indians. Smith established a friendly relationship with the Indians in the area. Then he arranged for one of the boys, Tom Savage, to live with them and learn to speak the Algonquian language. In exchange, a Powhatan boy named Namontack lived with the English for a while. The Indian boy eventually traveled to England with Captain Newport. Smith's idea worked. Savage later acted as a translator between the colonists and the Indians.

CHAPTER THREE

The Powhatan Confederacy

A Powerful Tribe

The Indians who had attacked the colonists when they first arrived at Chesapeake Bay were members of the Powhatan Confederacy. This was an empire of Algonquian-speaking tribes that lived in the Chesapeake Bay region. A powerful chief named Wahunsonacock ruled over about thirty tribes in the area. These included the Powhatan, Potomac, Pamunkey, Mattapony, and Chickahominy.

The tribes gave Wahunsonacock gifts of animal skins, corn, meat, and copper in order to win his favor. In return, Wahunsonacock gave gifts to tribal and village leaders in order to make them loyal to him. These leaders were known as *werowances*, an Algonquian word that means "he is rich."

Algonquian Indians built wigwams by bending branches into a dome to make a frame. Then they covered the frame with bark or grass mats.

Do You Speak Algonquian?

The Powhatan Indians did not just share their knowledge of planting and hunting with the English settlers. They also shared their language. Today, about 150 words in the English language come directly from the Algonquian language. That is more than from all other American Indian languages combined. These borrowed words include names for animals (*moose, chipmunk, raccoon, opossum,* and *skunk*), plants (*hickory, pecan,* and *squash*), foods (*hominy, succotash,* and *pone*), and everyday items such as *moccasin, tomahawk, wigwam,* and *papoose.*

The dialect that was spoken by the Powhatan Indians is sometimes called Virginia Algonkian. Most of the words now known from this extinct dialect come from notes made by colonists John Smith and William Strachey in the early 1600s.

Wahunsonacock was known as Powhatan by the English settlers because he was a member of and ruled over the Powhatan tribe. Because the tribes in Wahunsonacock's empire had similar languages and traditions, they are often referred to together as the Powhatan Indians. At the beginning of the seventeenth century, there were as many as 24,000 Powhatan living in some 200 villages in what is now known as the Tidewater region of Virginia.

The Powhatan were not surprised to see white men invading their land. They were not pleased to see them either. Four decades earlier, Spanish explorers had kidnapped a Powhatan boy, named him Don Luis, and taken him to Spain. There, he learned Spanish, attended school, and was baptized

Missionaries tried to convince the Powhatan and other Indians that they should adopt Christian beliefs.

as a Roman Catholic. When a group of Spanish **missionaries** came to America to try to make the Indians Christians, Don Luis came with them. Don Luis chose to live with his own people instead of the missionaries. When the Spanish demanded that he live with them and follow their religion, Don Luis refused. He launched an attack on the mission, killing everyone except for one boy. A year later, Spanish soldiers retaliated by killing thirty Indians. This disastrous introduction to Europeans was still fresh in the Powhatan's history. They were not about to welcome any Englishmen.

Powhatan Society

The Powhatan lived in a very structured society. The *werowances* were at the top of the ladder. Chief Powhatan had authority over all the tribal *werowances*, who in turn ruled over the village *werowances*. The *werowances* were the richest members of Powhatan society because other tribe members paid them **tribute**—gifts of food, copper, or animal skins. They lived in the biggest houses and ate the best food.

Second to the tribal *werowances* in power were the priests. The Powhatan believed that the priests could predict the future and control the weather. The priests advised the *werowances*. They also used their knowledge of plants to heal the sick and wounded.

One of the most important duties of the priests was to care for the village temples. Temples were often 100 feet

The Werowance

The title of *werowance* was inherited, passed down through the mother's side of the family. The oldest son was the first to serve as chief, followed by his younger brothers. After the youngest son's death, the oldest daughter became the *weronsqua*, the female leader of the tribe or village. Following the youngest daughter's death, the oldest daughter's firstborn son took on the responsibilities of *werowance*.

This drawing of Powhatan appeared in John Smith's book The Generall Historie of Virginia, New England, and the Summer Isles, *published in 1624. In the book, Smith told of his adventures in America.*

(30 meters) long. They held the bodies of *werowances* who had died, as well as offerings made to Okewas, the main god of the Powhatan. One room in the temple was used to store the tribute paid to the *werowance*.

The best hunters and warriors in each village served as advisers to the *werowances*. War councils were made up of these advisers, the *werowances*, and the priests.

Women's Roles

Living in a Powhatan village required everyone to do a fair share of work. Most tasks were divided into women's work and men's work. Children, even the youngest ones, were expected to help their parents with whatever needed to be done.

Women had a wide range of responsibilities. They farmed, wove baskets and mats, prepared animal hides for clothing, and made their own utensils and tools. They cooked all the meals. The women also built the longhouses and moved them when the villagers traveled between their winter and summer homes.

Corn was the primary crop of the Powhatan. The women planted four types, each of which ripened at a different time. Squash, beans, and pumpkins were planted around the corn. Tobacco was grown for use in tribal ceremonies. It was planted in its own field, away from the corn and other vegetables.

The women gathered strawberries, raspberries, apples, and grapes in the spring and summer. In the fall, walnuts, chestnuts, acorns, and other nuts were harvested. Some nuts were dried for use during the winter. Oil from the nuts was used in medicines and for cooking.

A Shot for Food

The Powhatan women helped their sons to learn to shoot bows and arrows accurately. Each morning, the mothers would toss a handful of moss into the air. The boys had to shoot it with their arrows. Otherwise, they would not be given breakfast.

Men's Roles

The Powhatan men hunted and fished to provide meat for the tribe. They used several different fishing techniques. Sometimes they fished from canoes, dragging nets made from deer sinew (tendons) or tree bark through the water. In shallow water, the men hunted large fish with spears, or they used hooks made of bone attached to thin ropes to make fishing reels. The men also built weirs at narrow places in the rivers. By laying stones in a V-shape across the river, they guided fish into the weirs.

Powhatan men hunted deer for the tribe. The women of the tribe butchered the deer and used the skin to make clothes and moccasins.

The men hunted many different types of game, including beavers, otters, bears, muskrats, rabbits, squirrels, and wild turkeys. Deer were the most widely hunted, providing meat as well as skins for clothing. Deer were so important that the whole village packed up and followed the deer west in the winter months.

The Powhatan often hunted deer in groups. When a herd of deer was found in an open area, some of the men spread out around the herd. They each built a small fire so that the deer were nearly surrounded by flames. Frightened, the deer would leap through the openings left between the fires. There, hunters waiting with bows and arrows would be ready to shoot. In wooded areas, it was more difficult to shoot deer. A hunter would often cover himself in a deerskin with the head still attached. This disguise let him get close enough to get a clear shot.

Besides hunting and fishing, Powhatan men worked on dugout canoes. Making canoes took a lot of time. First, a small fire was built at the base of the tree to be cut down. Once the tree was down, the branches were stripped off with axes. Then small fires were built on top of the log. From time to time, the men scraped out the burnt wood with stone axes and shells until the log had been shaped into a canoe. One of the longest canoes made in this way stretched 50 feet (15 meters) from end to end.

The Power of Copper

In Powhatan's eyes, copper was more valuable than gold. He gave gifts of copper ornaments and beads to ensure the loyalty of the chiefs he ruled. Copper was also used when trading with other tribes.

Most of Powhatan's copper came from the Midwest. Traders had to cross through the central Piedmont region of Virginia in order to trade with the Powhatan. The Monacan Indians, sworn enemies of the Powhatan, lived in this area. When the English colonists appeared in the early seventeenth century, the Powhatan were at war with the Monacans and could not get copper from the region.

The colonists brought sheets of copper and a jeweler who could fashion the copper into beads and other ornaments. Now the colonists could produce items that would be attractive to Powhatan and the chiefs under his control. Some scholars believe that Powhatan allowed the struggling colony to grow because he wanted this new supply of copper.

Making war was also a man's job. The Powhatan usually attacked other tribes to avenge some previous attack or to gain control of new territory. Sometimes, their goal was to kidnap women and children to adopt into their village. The Powhatan typically staged quick raids against their enemies. In most cases, only a few men were killed. They were horrified and disgusted that the British colonists would kill everyone, even women and children, in an attack.

Taking a Break

Although the Powhatan worked hard, they also believed that people needed time to relax and enjoy life. This idea was quite frustrating to the English. They did not understand why the Indians would not agree to work harder. The colonists wanted the natives to grow more corn for them in return for payments of beads or metal utensils. This difference between the two cultures contributed greatly to the growing tensions between them.

In the evenings, the Indians often enjoyed music and dancing. Musical instruments included reed flutes, deerskin drums, and gourd rattles. Men, women, and children alike enjoyed playing games, especially a type of football. The rules of the game varied depending upon which group was playing. Competitions that demonstrated physical ability, such as wrestling and foot racing, were also popular.

Dressing Up

The Tidewater region has warm summers and cool winters. Because the temperatures were moderate, the Powhatan wore little clothing until winter. From spring through fall, men and women wore loincloths made from grass or animal skins around their hips. Deerskin leggings and moccasins were worn during hunting trips and by members of a war party. In the winter, people rubbed oil into their skin to help them keep warm. Clothing made of animal skins was worn only on the coldest days.

The Powhatan had very distinctive hairstyles when the English first met them. Men shaved the right side of their heads so that the hair would not get tangled with their bows. The hair on the left side was left long, greased with walnut oil, and tied in a knot. Some men added feathers, antlers, or other decorations to the knot. (By the end of the sixteenth century, most Powhatan carried guns rather than bows. Because of this change, the men no longer shaved their heads.)

Girls were allowed to grow their hair very long in the back, but it was cut quite short in the front and on the sides. Once women married, they wore their hair in one of two styles. Some women cut their hair to one length just below the ears. Other women wore short bangs with a long braid down the back.

Virginia Tides

The Tidewater region of Virginia stretches along the Atlantic coast and extends inland about 100 miles (160 kilometers). Its name comes from the fact that the ocean's tides affect the rivers of the area, mixing saltwater with the fresh. Many of the streams and rivers in this region bear the names of the native people who lived there when the colonists arrived.

Powhatan society was very aware of class. Jewelry and other accessories were a way of demonstrating one's place in society. Small shells were often made into beads. These were fashioned into earrings, necklaces, and headbands and sewn onto robes and other items of clothing. Copper beads or headbands were worn only by the most powerful *werowances*.

John Smith spent much time learning about the Powhatan and other tribes. His successful relationships with the Indians helped Virginia's first colonists survive.

Both men and women pierced their ears. The showiest earrings, made from birds' feet or bear claws, were worn by the men. Men and women painted their faces and bodies. Only the women wore tattoos, however. The designs, often featuring flowers and animals, were created by rubbing soot into cuts made by a hot knife.

John Smith spent more time among the Powhatan than any other colonist. He included descriptions of the Indians' ways of life in many of his reports and books. This is his description of the Powhatan's finery.

[The Virginia Indians] adorne themselves most with copper beads and paintings. Their women...have their legs, hands...and face cunningly imbrodered with diverse workes, as beasts, serpentes [snakes], artificially wrought into their flesh with blacke spots [tattoos]. In each eare commonly they have 3 great holes, whereat they hang chaines bracelets or copper. Some of their men weare in those holes, a smal greene and yellow coloured snake, neare halfe a yard in length, which crawling and lapping her selfe about his necke often times familiarly would kisse his lips.

CHAPTER FOUR

The Growth of Jamestown

Trying to Survive

The first summer in Jamestown was a horrible experience for the colonists. Even though there were many animals in the forests, the colonists were not good hunters. As a result, they often went hungry. In addition, many died from dysentery and other diseases. Those who survived were often too weak to plant crops or work in the fields. The few healthy men were not interested in farming. Instead, they spent their time looking for gold. During this time, the colonists lived on crabs and a fish called sturgeon.

By September, only fifty of the original 105 settlers were still alive. Although the other leaders preferred to remain

By 1608, the Jamestown colonists had built houses, storage buildings, and a palisade to surround their settlement.

within the settlement or go out searching for gold, John Smith tried to trade with the Powhatan for corn. He had spent a great deal of time trading with and learning about the Indians. But because of a severe dry spell in the region, the Indians had even less corn than usual. They were not willing to share it with Smith and the colonists.

While on a hunting and trading trip in December, Smith was captured by Chief Powhatan's brother, Opechancanough. Smith was eventually taken to Powhatan's village. There, Smith thought the Powhatan warriors were going to kill him. The chief's daughter, Pocahontas, threw herself over Smith's body as he lay on the ground. Smith believed her actions saved his life.

Today, it is widely believed that Powhatan was actually conducting a ceremony and that he would not have killed Smith. He thought of Smith as the chief of the English tribe and wanted him alive so he could give Powhatan gifts like the other tribal chiefs. Smith did not understand the Indian ceremony and thought his life was in danger.

Fish Fry

Sturgeon can weigh up to 800 pounds (360 kilograms) and reach lengths of 15 feet (4.5 meters). John Smith noted that his men had seen "fish lying so thicke with their heads above the water, as for want of nets (our barge driving amongst them) we attempted to catch them with a frying pan, but we found it a bad instrument to catch fish with."

Pocahontas begged Powhatan to spare John Smith's life.

Smith returned to Jamestown on January 2, 1608. There, he found only thirty-eight men still alive. Sick and desperate, they were determined to sail the ship *Discovery* back to England. Smith vowed to fire cannons at the ship until it sank if they tried to board it. The outraged colonists threatened Smith's life. Just in the nick of time, Captain Newport returned from England and sailed up the river with fresh supplies and sixty new colonists.

Many colonists hated John Smith. But the governing council finally recognized that he had the skills necessary to help the struggling colony survive. He was elected president of the governing council in 1608.

Smith soon cracked down on those who thought they shouldn't be made to work. He announced, "He that will not work, neither shall he eat." Soon, the colonists were working six hours a day in the fields and the forts. Although this discipline most likely saved their lives that winter, the colonists' resentment of Smith continued to grow.

A Lazy Workforce

John Smith was fed up with the colonists who came to Jamestown unwilling to work. In a letter to the Virginia Company, he pleaded, "When you send again, I entreat you rather send but thirty carpenters, husbandmen, gardeners, fishermen, blacksmiths, masons, and diggers up of trees' roots, well provided, than a thousand of such as we have."

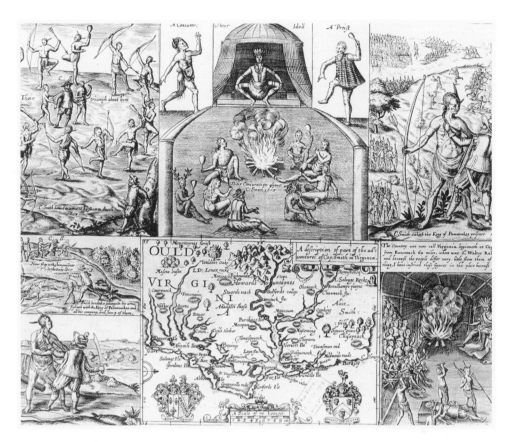

This drawing appeared in one of John Smith's books. It shows his many adventures in the New World.

A year later, Smith's leg was badly burned when some gunpowder blew up nearby. When a ship arrived in Jamestown with 400 new colonists that fall, he was forced to return to England until he healed. Smith never went back to Virginia, although he did explore New England several years later.

The Starving Time

After John Smith's departure, the colony had a hard time. The population of Jamestown now stood at 500. For the first time, women were part of the settlement. Trouble loomed, since winter was not far away and supplies were already running low with the new mouths to feed. Without Smith there to negotiate with the Indians for corn, the colonists tried threats.

Tired of being asked to feed the colonists, the Powhatan struck back. By the winter of 1609, the colonists were virtual prisoners inside their palisade. Although they had plenty of pigs and other domestic animals nearby, the settlers could not reach them without being shot at by the Powhatan.

The cold winds that winter cut right through the settlers' clothing. To keep fires going, the buildings within the fort were slowly torn apart and burned. After exhausting their meager supply of food, the colonists turned to whatever they could find inside the fort. Rats, snakes, horses, and even horsehide became meals for the desperate settlers. One man even killed and ate his wife. (He was later convicted of murder and burned at the stake.)

When a supply ship reached Jamestown in May 1610, only sixty of the 500 colonists were still alive. After hearing of the horrifying winter, the newly arrived colonists did not

Strict Rules

Under Governor Dale's command, everyone in Jamestown worked hard. The punishment for breaking a rule, swearing, or refusing to work was a whipping. Anyone who received three whippings was executed.

The colonists were forbidden to gamble or play dice. However, **archaeologists** have found several dice, no bigger than a pencil eraser, on the site of the original fort of Jamestown. Made of bone or ivory, the small dice were easy to hide. A small lead figure of a boy dancing has also been recovered. Some speculate that the figure is a toy. Others think it might have been made for trading purposes.

want to stay and the survivors were ready to abandon Jamestown. The boats were loaded and set sail for England. But before they reached the mouth of the James River, they were met by Lord de La Warr. De La Warr had been appointed the new governor of Jamestown. He had with him 300 new settlers. De La Warr was determined that the colony would be successful under his leadership. He made the ships turn around and return to Jamestown.

Lord de La Warr placed the colony under martial law, meaning soldiers helped enforce the laws. Both De La Warr and the next governor, Sir Thomas Dale, were very strict, but under their leadership, Jamestown began to grow. Colonists still died, but rarely from starvation. Even the colonists' relationship with the Powhatan improved.

Green Gold

Among the many challenges facing the Virginia Company was how to make a profit. The company had been sending thousands of colonists to the New World, but it had little to show for its investment. In fact, the company was dangerously close to losing all its money. Then a new crop brought prosperity to Virginia. Tobacco was gaining popularity in Europe, but the native tobacco grown in Virginia was not of very high quality.

In 1614, a colonist named John Rolfe brought some tobacco seeds from the West Indies to Jamestown. The crop flourished, and two years later, 2,500 pounds (1,125 kilograms) of tobacco were shipped to England from Virginia. Demand for American tobacco skyrocketed. By the 1660s, Virginia was shipping 10 million pounds (4.5 million kilograms) of tobacco each year.

Tobacco quickly became so valuable that its leaves were used as money. Wages were paid with tobacco leaves,

Health vs. Wealth

King James was less than enthusiastic when the Virginia colonists began growing tobacco. He described smoking as "a custom loathsome to the eye, hateful to the nose, harmful to the brain, [and] dangerous to the lungs." As the demand for Virginia tobacco grew, however, James dropped his objections. After all, taxes on the imported tobacco provided a great deal of the king's income.

and colonists paid their debts and taxes with the leaves. Tobacco became known as "green gold."

Raising tobacco was hard work. Fields had to be cleared of trees. After the tobacco was planted, it needed constant care. Once the leaves were harvested, they had to be dried and packed. Since the tobacco used up the nutrients in the soil very quickly, a field could be used for only a few years. Then another field had to be cleared. Tobacco farmers and plantation owners needed help with this backbreaking work. For many years, they used indentured servants. Later, slaves were purchased to work on the plantations. Even small farmers who could afford them bought one or two slaves.

Tobacco plantations required large groups of slaves to do the difficult work of planting, tending, and harvesting the tobacco crop.

Colonial homes were very different from modern houses. Simple activities like getting a glass of water or washing clothes could require a lot of work. Colonial children spent much of their time doing chores.

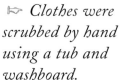

☞ Most colonial homes had at least one cat to catch mice and rats.

☞ Clothes were scrubbed by hand using a tub and washboard.

☞ Water came from a well outside the house and was carried inside in buckets.

✄ A hand-powered pump brought water from the well to the trough for farm animals to drink.

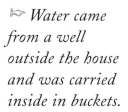

✄ Most work was done by hand. This included carrying heavy loads of lumber or other materials

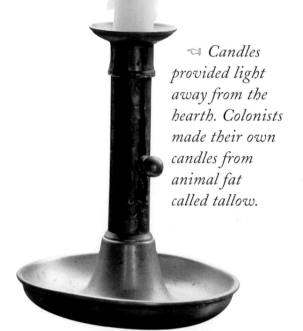

🐚 Candles provided light away from the hearth. Colonists made their own candles from animal fat called tallow.

🔥 The fireplace or hearth was the center of most colonial homes. Firewood had to be chopped and carried inside every day. The ashes from the fire were shoveled from the hearth and carried outside.

🍃 Seeds and stems had to be removed from cotton before it was spun into thread and made into cloth.

🔥 Colonial women and girls spent hours spinning cotton, flax, and wool into thread and yarn to make clothes.

59

CHAPTER FIVE
Turning Points

Change in the Air

Many changes had occurred in the colony of Virginia between 1607 and 1618. There were now four settlements. The colonists were learning to grow tobacco. In 1614, Pocahontas married John Rolfe, a successful tobacco farmer. As a result of their marriage, the Powhatan and colonists agreed to live in peace.

Some things did not change, though. The colonists were still relying upon the Native Americans for much of their food. Rather than "wasting" their land growing corn and other vegetables, the colonists wanted to plant tobacco. As in the past, the Indians did not supply as much as the colonists wanted, either because their crops were not large enough or they wanted to feed their own families. The colonists often responded by killing the Indians.

Pocahontas, the daughter of the Powhatan chief, married colonist John Rolfe in 1614. She later traveled with him to England.

Faced with increasing disapproval in England, the Virginia Company made several changes in 1619. The company announced that 50 acres (20 hectares) of land would be given to settlers who paid their own way to America. Settlers would receive an additional 50 acres for every family member or servant whose passage they paid for.

The first assembly of the House of Burgesses met in Jamestown in 1619. It was the first time lawmakers were elected in America.

Thus, a family of four who brought two servants with them received 300 acres (120 hectares) of land. Investors in the company received 100 acres (40 hectares) of land. Even indentured servants were promised 50 acres (20 hectares) of land when their contracts ended. Suddenly, the colonists were motivated to work hard. Since they were now landowners, any profits from successful crops went into their pockets, not anyone else's.

Governmental changes were also in store. The Virginia Company had been heavily criticized for its harsh laws and punishments. In 1619, the company announced that the colony would now be governed by the Virginia General Assembly. This new legislative body was made up of the governor, the Governor's Council, and the House of Burgesses. While the governor and the Governor's Council were appointed, the representatives to the House of Burgesses were elected by the people living in Virginia. During this period, only white men who owned land could vote. Still, the Virginia House of Burgesses was the first representative government in America.

A Demand for Labor

One of the first laws passed by the House of Burgesses required colonists to grow enough food in addition to tobacco and other cash crops they grew. Other laws supported the Anglican Church by requiring colonists to attend church services, avoid swearing, and give up gambling. Property owners convicted of any of these sins were punished by fines, but servants and apprentices were often whipped.

The House of Burgesses met regularly to make laws for the colony. Although any laws it suggested had to be approved by the governor, the burgesses had a great deal of influence. This change was the first step toward self-government. The last step would take place over a century later, when the colonies banded together to fight a war for independence.

An air of excitement spread through Europe as these changes became known. The opportunity to own land and take control of their destiny drew thousands of men and women to Virginia. In 1619 alone, 1,200 colonists arrived in Virginia. This marked the beginning of the period known as "the Great Migration."

The Beginning of Slavery

The opportunities for land ownership and self-government that opened up in 1619 did much to shape the future development of the United States. But another significant change that same year would take a terrible toll on the developing colony and eventually the new nation.

In August 1619, a Dutch slave ship arrived in Jamestown's harbor. The crew was running low on supplies. The sailors asked for food in exchange for the twenty or so African slaves they had on board. These first blacks were treated just like indentured servants. After serving out their contracts, they were given clothing, tools, and land. Some free blacks eventually bought their own indentured servants to work on their farms.

Although blacks were now living in Virginia, a system of slavery did not develop immediately. For one thing, slaves were quite expensive. Since many people died at a young age from diseases that spread through the colony, many farmers did not want to spend large amounts of money on slaves who might die within a few years. It was cheaper to purchase indentured servants.

Slaves were brought to Jamestown from Africa and sold in Virginia for the first time in 1619.

Over time, however, several factors led to a reliance on slaves rather than indentured servants. First, tobacco prices dropped. In order to continue making a profit, farmers had to cut their costs. About this time, the price of slaves dropped. Owning slaves who never had to be paid and who had to work for their entire lives was now cheaper than purchasing five to seven years of an indentured servant's labor. Additionally, the children of slaves would automatically be slaves as well. Since fewer indentured servants were immigrating at this point, many owners of large plantations switched from servants to slaves. The owners of small farms also started using slave labor in order to stay competitive.

A Closer Look at the Transatlantic Slave Trade

In the fifteenth and sixteenth centuries, many Spanish colonies were established in the Americas. Central and South America had large deposits of gold and silver that the Spanish wanted to mine. In the Caribbean, the rich soil was perfect for large sugar plantations. The only thing missing was large numbers of people to do the work. At first, the Spanish used the Native Americans who lived in these regions as slaves. However, disease and overwork killed most of them. So the Spanish began to import slave labor from Africa.

Slaves were captured and taken from their villages in Africa. They were brought to the coast by slave traders and put on ships bound for America.

Decades later, England established its own colonies in North America. In the southern colonies, crops such as tobacco, rice, and sugar required many laborers. Eventually, African slaves were brought to America.

European slave traders followed a triangular route that was called the "Triangle Trade." The slave ships traveled from Europe to West Africa, where they were loaded with slaves. The Middle Passage, a voyage lasting six to eight weeks, took the slaves from Africa to the Americas. In the Americas, the slaves were unloaded and sold at auctions. Then the ships were loaded with goods produced in the colonies before they returned to Europe.

The Middle Passage

The Middle Passage was a horrifying experience for the Africans aboard the ship. Only months earlier, these men, women, and children had been living normal lives in their villages. Then suddenly they were snatched away from their families. Some were captured during tribal wars. Others were kidnapped by slave traders. All of them found themselves tied together with rope and crowded into a dark prison near the Atlantic coast.

When a slave ship arrived in Africa, the captain would row ashore to inspect the slaves. Marks called brands were burned into their skins to identify them as slaves. Leg irons were fastened around their ankles. They were then herded aboard the small boats that would take them to the waiting slave ship. Some threw themselves overboard at the first opportunity. Sure that they would never see their homes or families again, they chose to die rather than be forced into slavery.

The Growth of Slavery in Virginia

Year	Number of Slaves
1619	20
1650	300
1671	2,000
1700	6,000
1730	28,500
1750	60,000
1790	292,627

Some slaves jumped overboard to escape slavery. They often drowned before reaching shore.

The voyage from Africa to the Americas was miserable for the slaves. Many slave traders crowded the slaves so tightly together in the hold of a ship that they had little room to move. It was hot and dirty in the belly of the ship. Many of the slaves suffered from seasickness. Diseases such as dysentery and smallpox killed many of the slaves during the passage. When the weather permitted, the slaves were brought up to the deck and forced to exercise in the fresh air.

The transatlantic slave trade lasted for nearly four centuries. During that time, an estimated 20 million Africans were sold into slavery.

The Great Massacre of 1622

Thousands of new colonists poured into Virginia each year. Every acre of land they claimed was land that had once been settled and hunted by the Powhatan Indians. Much of this land was now being cleared and planted. The Indians' traditional way of life was in danger.

Child Labor

Powhatan children were sometimes sent to work as servants for the colonists. They were supposed to be free to return to their tribes when they reached the age of twenty-five. However, some colonists failed to honor this agreement. Sometimes, the colonists did not even wait for native parents to send their children to settlements. Instead, the colonists kidnapped the children and claimed that the parents had sent them to be servants.

After Powhatan died in 1618, his brother Opechancanough became the ruler of the Powhatan Confederacy. He was very angry about the way the settlers had treated the Indians. In 1622, Opechancanough planned to attack and kill the settlers in his territory.

The chief sent groups of Indian warriors to visit plantations and settlements throughout the region. Because recent relations with the Indians had been friendly, the settlers did not suspect that the Indians intended to attack them. When the Powhatan struck, nearly 350 colonists were killed. The death toll would have been higher if not for an Indian boy named Chango.

Chango told the settlers in Jamestown about the planned attacks. Thanks to his warning, fewer than a third of the Jamestown settlers were killed.

Opechancanough believed that the English would give up and leave America after the **massacre**. Instead, the English tried their best to wipe out the Powhatan tribes. During the fall, they "cut down crops, smashed canoes," destroyed temples, "burned villages, and killed any Indians they came across." These actions left the Powhatan to try to survive the winter without food or shelter. Unfortunately, the English also attacked Indian tribes that had not taken part in the massacre.

Chief Opechancanough convinced other Indians to attack the Virginia colonists in 1622.

After a year of fighting, the Indians and the English agreed to meet to discuss a peace treaty. At the end of the talks, the English offered the Indians a drink of wine to celebrate their truce. After drinking, about 200 Indians collapsed. The English had poisoned their wine. As the Indians tried to escape, the settlers killed them. Opechancanough survived the massacre, and the fighting continued for another ten years.

After more than twenty years of fighting, Opechancanough was captured and killed by the colonists in 1646.

A Royal Colony

Dismayed at the bloodbath triggered by the massacre of the Powhatan, King James took control of Virginia in 1624. He announced that it would now be a royal colony. This meant that the king himself would make decisions regarding the colony's government and settlement.

One of the king's first orders was to put an end to the House of Burgesses. The colonists were angry about this loss of control over their government. Aware of their resentment, the governor of the colony often sought the "advice" of the elected representatives in informal gatherings. The House of Burgesses would be restored when a new king took the throne in 1639.

Under the direction of King James, wealthy landowners continued to gain power in Virginia. Unlike the other colonies that were being founded in America, Virginia had few towns. Instead, most Virginians lived on farms and plantations. Whenever possible, these were located on the banks of rivers to make it easier to ship tobacco to market.

Matchmaking in Virginia in 1619

Single men and families were not the only people interested in settling in Virginia. A bride-ship carrying nearly a hundred single women who wished to marry arrived in Jamestown in 1619. Each prospective groom had to pay 120 pounds (54 kilograms) of tobacco to cover the cost of his new wife's voyage.

The End of the Powhatan Confederacy

By 1640, the Virginia settlers outnumbered the Powhatan almost two to one. At this time, Opechancanough was nearly blind and unable to walk on his own. Despite his disability, he organized another surprise attack against the colonists in 1644. Four hundred settlers were killed. The British struck back with a **vengeance**, destroying all the nearby Indian villages. Many of the Indian survivors fled to the north and west. Those who remained in Virginia were forced to live on small reservations (land set aside for the Indians). Laws were passed making it legal for colonists to shoot any Indian who entered an English settlement without permission.

Opechancanough was captured in 1646. Before he could be transported to England, a soldier shot him in the back and killed him. By 1649, the powerful Powhatan Confederacy was in shambles. With their hunting grounds and fields destroyed, many of the Indians had to work for the settlers in order to survive.

The Human Cost of Colonization

By the mid-1600s, Virginia was recognized as a successful colony. This success had come at a great price, however. By 1622, only 2,000 of the first 10,000 colonists who arrived in Virginia were still alive. In that year, one English writer claimed that Virginia was becoming known more as a slaughterhouse than as a plantation. And he did not even consider the cost suffered by the Powhatan and the African slaves.

The Powhatan, who had helped the first colonists survive, were severely reduced in number. This was due to both disease and ongoing hostilities with the English. Less than four decades after the English arrived in America, the Powhatan population had shrunk from 24,000 to 5,000. Much of the natives' land was being taken over by English settlers anxious to get rich growing tobacco. Soon, slave ships would be bringing thousands of Africans to Virginia.

The Virginia Pilgrims?

In 1620, a group of pilgrims seeking religious freedom set sail for Virginia. Their boat, the *Mayflower*, went off course during the voyage. After landing in present-day Massachusetts, the Pilgrims were too exhausted to travel on to Virginia. Instead, they founded the settlement of Plymouth, Massachusetts.

CHAPTER SIX

Expanding the Colony

A Split Society

Virginia was fast developing three levels of society. At the top were the Tidewater plantation owners. They owned hundreds or thousands of acres of land that had made them quite rich. They were favored by the English governors, who appointed the landowners to the Governor's Council of the General Assembly. There, they made laws to enrich themselves. They lowered taxes on large estates while raising taxes on smaller farms.

The middle level of society was made up of the small farmers. Many of these were former indentured servants. They had discovered something far more valuable than

In the early 1700s, wealthy Virginians went to church dressed in their finest clothes.

Virginia's House of Burgesses and General Court met in the colonial capitol building in Williamsburg beginning in 1705.

sheer wealth in Virginia. They had found independence. Independence meant they no longer had to depend upon others for their livelihoods. With land of their own, their success was based on their willingness to work hard. Anything that could cause them to lose their land and their independence, such as high taxes and low tobacco prices, caused a great deal of worry.

At the bottom of society were the growing numbers of black slaves. They had no control over their own lives. While early slaves had the opportunity to earn money and purchase their freedom, this right had disappeared by the 1670s. By 1705, Virginia laws declared that all servants who had not been Christians in their native country would now be slaves. Slaves could not be taught to read or write. Slaves could not travel anywhere without a written pass. Slaves could not gather in groups of more than four outside of the plantation. Although they had once had the same hopes for freedom as indentured whites, black slaves were now legally considered to be real estate.

Plantation Life

The plantations of Virginia were so large that they were like small, self-contained villages. The families who lived on these plantations fell into two distinct categories. The wealthy plantation owners enjoyed lives of luxury and leisure. Their lifestyle was made possible by the slaves who lived on the plantation.

The owners' families lived in large, graceful manor houses that were often built of brick. Wide, tree-lined roads led to the front doors. Inside, the rooms were large and elegantly decorated. The furnishings were often imported from Europe, as were the latest fashions in clothes. Household items and clothing were both carefully selected, since they were considered a symbol of wealth.

Plantation owners entertained frequently, hosting dances or concerts for their wealthy friends. Because there was such a great distance between plantations, the visitors often stayed for a week or more. The entertainment focused more on the adults than the children. Horseback riding, card games, hunting, and horse races were all favorite activities.

The children who grew up in a manor house were quite spoiled. They were dressed like small adults. Their toys allowed them to practice the roles they would inherit when they grew up. Girls played with china tea sets and dressed their dolls in silk and velvet. Toy soldiers, marbles, and fancy tops were among the boys' favorite playthings. The children were cared for by servants who helped them dress, supervised their meals, and put them to bed.

Most planters hired private teachers to educate their sons. Older boys were sometimes sent to England to continue their education or attended William and Mary College after its founding in Williamsburg, Virginia, in 1693. Many people of that time did not believe that girls

A Capital Move

In 1699, the capital of Virginia was moved from Jamestown to Williamsburg. In addition to numerous stores and government buildings, the new capital boasted the first college in Virginia. The College of William and Mary, founded in 1693, is the second-oldest college in America.

needed to learn to read and write. Instead, they were taught handiwork such as embroidery. Both boys and girls learned important social skills such as dancing and horseback riding.

In the 1700s, plantation owners also looked forward to attending the Publick Times that were held in Williamsburg twice a year. This was a time when people came to town to do business with the courts. Since so many people came to the capital city during Publick Times, plantation owners were able to conduct any business they might have with other planters. The women enjoyed shopping at the many stores. And there were gala events such as balls and theater productions to attend.

Life as a Slave

Behind the manor houses, tucked out of sight, was the other side of plantation life. By the eighteenth century, this face was overwhelmingly black. African slaves had become the backbone of the Tidewater plantations.

Slaves planted and harvested the tobacco and then built barrels to ship it in. Slaves shaped the nails and lumber that kept the plantation buildings in good condition. Slaves raised the food, cooked and served the meals, drove the carriages, and kept the manor houses spotless. Slaves made iron tools, soap, candles, shoes, and woolen and linen cloth. Their reward was to live to do the same the next day.

Slavery in the Cradle of Liberty

The most glaring contradiction in Virginia's history is the fact that many of the country's founders who argued for freedom and liberty were Virginia slave owners. Thomas Jefferson, who wrote that "all men are created equal," owned anywhere from 200 to 600 slaves at a time.

Although George Washington and Jefferson owned slaves, they did speak out in favor of abolishing slavery. Because slavery was so much a part of Virginia's plantation economy, however, everyone feared financial ruin if slaves were set free.

The slaves lived in very different conditions from their owners. Located close to the fields, each slave cabin typically housed nine or ten people. They slept on old blankets spread over the dirt floor. The cabins usually had a fireplace for cooking and to warm the room in the winter. Small windows allowed some light and fresh air into the cabin.

The slaves who worked in the fields rose before dawn. They were expected to tend the tobacco plants from sunup to sundown. During this time, they were allowed only a few short breaks and a small meal. At harvest time, the slaves were often required to sort tobacco leaves or husk corn in the evenings. It was backbreaking work, and any hint of defiance would result in a whipping of thirty lashes or worse punishment.

Some slaves were chosen to work in the manor houses. They were generally given nicer clothes and treated more kindly. The cooks worked in a kitchen set apart from the main house. The separate kitchen kept the heat from the fires, as well as the cooking smells, out of the house. It also reduced the chance that a fire in the kitchen would spread to the main house.

Slave children helped out in the gardens and cared for the pigs, chickens, and cows. Older children watched after the younger ones. Older children often worked alongside the skilled craftsmen on the plantation, learning the art of blacksmithing or weaving.

Many plantation owners believed that the only way to motivate their slaves to work hard was through fear. A slave who lied to a master might have an ear nailed to a post for an hour. When the time was up, the ear was cut off. Slaves who ran away were whipped. If they ran away more than once, their toes might be cut off. Sometimes, slaves were beaten so brutally that they died. When this happened, the owners were not punished. According to the law, the owners had not done anything wrong.

Hard Times

Tobacco brought wealth and prosperity to many Virginia colonists in the first half of the seventeenth century. The prospect of getting rich in Virginia brought many new immigrants to the colony.

Governor Berkeley was popular with rich plantation owners because he gave them special privileges.

After the middle of the century, however, these new arrivals faced an uphill battle when they tried to make a living growing tobacco. Most of the Tidewater land was already settled. The land that was available had no easy access to rivers. The new farmers had to spend more to get their tobacco to market. They also paid higher colonial taxes than the plantation owners. This meant that the small farmers made less money on each pound of tobacco they raised than the wealthy Tidewater plantation owners did.

In the 1660s, the king ruled that the colonists had to sell all their tobacco to England. Since English tobacco merchants did not have to compete against other traders for the crop, prices plunged. They fell lower still when millions of tons of tobacco reached England. With so much tobacco available, it became very cheap.

Suddenly, the small farmers were in a bind. It cost them more to raise an acre of tobacco than they could sell it for. Many found themselves in debt, unable to pay their taxes. Their land was auctioned off, usually to one of the plantation owners. Many small farmers blamed the wealthy colonists for causing these hardships. Tensions between the two groups ran high.

The governor of Virginia, William Berkeley, made the problem worse. He believed that Virginia should have strict social classes, just like England. He disapproved of the idea that indentured servants and "common men" could become landowners and improve their lot in life. Berkeley therefore gave special treatment to wealthy plantation owners. Some were given licenses to trade with the Indians for furs. Others received large **grants** of land on the frontier.

Berkeley's land grants caused problems for the indentured servants who completed their contracts in the 1660s and beyond. The former servants were owed land for their services, but there was little available in central Virginia. These men faced a difficult choice. They could give up their dreams of owning land and become **tenant farmers** on one of the large plantations. Or they could move to the frontier, where violent clashes with the Indians were common. Many chose to settle the frontier. There, their anger at the unfair treatment they had received fueled a rebellion against Berkeley.

William Berkeley did not believe that all men were created equal. In fact, he had little regard for anyone who was not wealthy. He believed that small property owners and servants should welcome the opportunity to work for the large plantation owners. Many of his policies were intended to slow the settlement of the frontier so that the plantation owners would have access to more workers.

Bacon's Rebellion

In the 1670s, the settlers on the frontier were frequently attacked by Susquehannock Indians. These natives did not want any European colonists moving into their land. The settlers asked Governor Berkeley to send the militia (a group of citizen soldiers) to the frontier to protect them. Berkeley refused. The settlers asked for permission to kill all the Indians in the area themselves. Again, Berkeley refused, in large part because he and his wealthy supporters were growing rich as they traded for furs with the Indians. Furious, the settlers accused Berkeley of caring more about protecting the fur trade than defending their lives.

Nathaniel Bacon and his followers drove Governor Berkeley from Jamestown.

Nathaniel Bacon, a wealthy young planter who lived on the frontier, led the settlers in vicious attacks against the Indians. He also gave fiery speeches demanding better lands for freed servants and lower taxes. His followers included poor freedmen (former servants), indentured servants, and slaves.

In 1676, Berkeley accused Bacon of treason. Bacon responded by leading a group of armed followers to Jamestown to confront the governor. When Berkeley fled the city, Bacon burned the statehouse (capitol) to the ground. The rebellion ended when Bacon died suddenly of dysentery. Governor Berkeley returned to Jamestown and then arrested and hanged twenty-three of Bacon's supporters.

A New Partnership

One surprising outcome of Bacon's Rebellion was a stronger relationship between the plantation owners and the small farmers. After the rebellion, King Charles II grew concerned that the high taxes imposed by the colonial government were lessening his share of tobacco profits. He sent Sir Herbert Jeffreys to take over as governor. Jeffreys's plan was to limit the power of the plantation owners by giving the small farmers more of a voice in the government. But before any major changes could take place, Jeffreys died.

Governor Alexander Spotswood explored the Virginia frontier and made treaties with the Iroquois that allowed settlers to move into western Virginia.

It was obvious to the plantation owners that their way of life would be at risk if the king became more involved in the colony's government. The General Assembly decided to take matters into its own hands. It began lowering the taxes paid by the small farmers and poor whites. The members of the assembly also began to promote the idea that they were protecting the rights of all free colonists, not just their own. Before long, the colonists were thinking of themselves as Virginians rather than as English people living in Virginia.

Moving Into the Mountains

As the eighteenth century began, most Virginians lived in the Tidewater region. Some settlers had claimed land in the central region known as the Piedmont. As immigrants continued to flood into the colony, however, the pressure to open up new lands for settlement grew stronger.

England discouraged movement westward. The English did not want to have to send soldiers into the wilderness to protect settlers from Indian attacks. But the Virginians began moving westward anyway. After all, Virginia's original charter did not specify any westward limit to its territory. As far as the Virginians were concerned, settling the frontier was their right.

In 1716, Governor Alexander Spotswood led an expedition to explore the Appalachian Mountains. He called his group "the Knights of the Golden Horseshoe." They traveled into the Blue Ridge Mountains. There, they found plentiful game, rich forests, and clear rivers. One of the most beautiful places they found was a river valley that the Indians called Shanando. Through the colonists' pronunciation, it became known as the Shenandoah River valley.

Spotswood's expedition set off a period of rapid growth in central and western Virginia. Thousands of German and Scotch-Irish settlers migrated from Pennsylvania to the Shenandoah Valley around the 1720s, attracted by relatively low land prices, fertile land, and some measure of religious freedom. They were joined by small numbers of French, Dutch, Swiss, and Swedish settlers.

By 1750, small farms dotted the Shenandoah Valley. Virginia's population had almost tripled in five decades. Most of the new arrivals lived on small farms on the frontier. Once again, settlers began to look west for new land. This time, they would venture beyond the Appalachians into Ohio country, setting off nine years of war between England and France.

The Scotch-Irish

— ᘯᘯ❈ᘯᘯ —

The term *Scotch-Irish* is somewhat misleading. It refers to Irish Protestants, most of Scottish descent, who emigrated to the colonies in the 1700s. The Scotch-Irish label came into use in the late 1800s, when these early settlers wanted to distinguish themselves from the flood of Irish Catholic immigrants.

Life on the Frontier

The families that settled Virginia's frontier were hardy, self-sufficient people. Everyone had to work hard every day to survive in the wilderness. The frontier families had to bring everything they needed with them or make it themselves. There were no towns in the Shenandoah Valley when they arrived. There were no nearby stores where they could purchase supplies. Most settlers lived isolated lives, although there were several German communities that had moved as a group into Virginia.

Most of the settlers cut down trees and used the logs to build rough cabins. The German settlers were more likely to build stone houses, however. Most settlers built simple tables, chairs, and other necessary furnishings as well. A cabin was typically a single room with a fireplace on one wall. Meals were cooked over the fireplace, and in the winter, it heated the cabin. Family members slept on mattresses stuffed with straw or cornhusks. Some cabins had a loft built over half the room to provide a sleeping area for the children.

The clearings where the logs had been harvested would become fields. Since most farmers did not have the necessary equipment or horses to pull tree stumps from the ground, crops were planted around them. Corn was the main crop on the small wilderness farms. The women also tended small vegetable gardens. Whenever possible, the settlers planted extra corn, hoping to trade it for other supplies after the harvest. Berries and nuts that grew wild in the woods were a special treat in the summer and fall.

A Rough Life

Settlers depended upon their hunting skills to supplement the food they raised. Men and boys did most of the hunting. (Women also learned to shoot, but hunting wasn't their main responsibility.) Small game such as rabbit and squirrels was a mainstay of the pioneers' diet, although deer and bear meat was highly valued. Extra meat was dried or smoked to preserve it for later use. In addition to shooting wild game, many farmers raised hogs and chickens.

Children were expected to help their parents with the many chores that needed to be done each day. They helped plant, weed, and harvest the corn and other vegetables. They also learned to shoot guns and hunt. Girls were taught how to sew and cook. There were no schools in the wilderness, so most children did not receive any education. The lucky ones had parents who had some education. These children learned to read, write, and cipher (do mathematical calculations).

Death at an early age was common on the frontier. Injuries could quickly become infected, and snakebites often proved fatal. Simple colds could easily turn into pneumonia. More serious diseases such as diphtheria and measles could kill an entire family. Families relied upon herbal remedies made from plants such as sassafras and tobacco and prayed for the best.

Although social occasions were limited, farm families would gather to help each other out at harvest or when a house or barn was built. These get-togethers allowed settlers to visit with their neighbors while they got major tasks done. While the men worked on the buildings and harvests, the women would quilt and cook. Children took advantage of the rare chance to play with others their age. Leapfrog and tag were two of their favorite games.

CHAPTER SEVEN

Growing Independence

The French and Indian War

As more and more colonists poured into Virginia, the need for land grew. Settlers began looking at Ohio country, the land between the Appalachian Mountains and the Mississippi River. In the mid-1700s, this territory was home to several Indian tribes. These tribes had been pushed off their traditional lands by earlier colonists. French fur traders also lived in the area, which was claimed by France.

In 1749, England claimed ownership of the rich lands in the Ohio Valley. France considered the territory to be French and began to build forts in northern Ohio to strengthen its claim. George Washington, a member of the Virginia militia, was sent to the area to convince the French to stop building

Townspeople of Winchester, Virginia, greeted Lieutenant George Washington as he led his troops to fight in the French and Indian War.

the forts. When they refused, Washington returned in 1754 with 150 troops and attacked the French. Although this first attack was successful, the French quickly struck back with a force of 900 soldiers and Indian allies. Washington surrendered, and the French allowed him to return to Virginia.

This battle was the first in the nine-year-long war that became known as the French and Indian War (1754–1763). When it ended, England controlled North America from the Atlantic coast west to the Mississippi River and from present-day Canada south to the Gulf of Mexico. France had lost all of its territory in the New World.

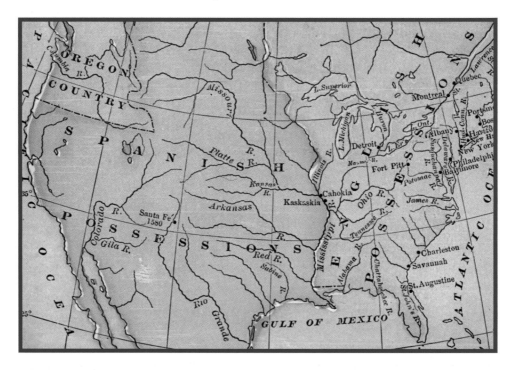

The territory in America controlled by the English after the French and Indian War is colored green.

Although the war was not fought in Virginia, its militia sent many men to fight in the war. When the war finally ended, George Washington had gained a reputation throughout the colonies for his leadership and bravery. And Virginia's colonists were ready to move into the newly claimed territory, despite Britain's orders not to settle there. The British had made a treaty with the Indian tribes west of the Appalachian Mountains not to settle that territory.

Uproar Over Taxes

The French and Indian War was very costly for Britain. It had to find a way to repay its debts. To raise money, Parliament (England's body of lawmakers) decided to tax the colonies.

In 1765, Parliament passed the Stamp Act. This law required merchants to purchase stamps and put them on every piece of printed paper, including newspapers and playing cards. The courts had to do the same for all official documents. The prices of newspapers would go up, as would the cost of doing business. All the colonies already had governing councils that imposed taxes. But the colonists had never been taxed directly by Parliament before. Outraged, they vowed "no taxation without representation." They thought they should not have to pay taxes when they had no representative in Parliament to speak for them.

In Virginia's House of Burgesses, Patrick Henry introduced seven **resolutions** critical of the Stamp Act. Henry could have been tried as a traitor because he directly challenged the king's power. However, the members of the Virginia assembly passed four of the resolutions. These declared that colonists in Virginia had the same rights as people in England and that the colonists had the right to be taxed only by their own representatives in the colonies. The governor did not agree. As a result, he did away with the House of Burgesses.

Famous Words

The Second Virginia Convention met in 1775 to select **delegates** for the Second Continental Congress. At the meeting, Patrick Henry suggested arming a militia to protect the colony from the English. Other delegates urged the convention to wait for a response from Parliament, in hopes that peace might be maintained. In response, Patrick Henry gave a speech that still rings today:

Gentlemen may cry, peace, peace—but there is no peace.

The war is actually begun! The next gale that sweeps from the north will bring to our ears the clash of resounding arms! Our brethren are already in the field! Why stand we here idle? What is it that gentlemen wish? What would they have? Is life so dear, or peace so sweet, as to be purchased at the price of chains and slavery? Forbid it, Almighty God! I know not what course others may take, but as for me, give me liberty or give me death!

People in other colonies were inspired by Virginia's actions. Riots broke out in many colonies. Tax collectors were threatened and harassed until they resigned. Colonists agreed to boycott English products, meaning they would not purchase these goods. Finally, Parliament gave in and repealed, or ended, the Stamp Act in 1766.

Rebellion

Parliament had not given up the idea of taxing the colonies. In 1767, it passed the Townshend Acts. These were taxes on English products such as tea, molasses, and glass. Once again, the colonies protested by refusing to buy anything from English merchants. Although it was illegal to import these products from other countries, some colonists smuggled them in. Eventually, Parliament repealed these taxes as well.

The colonists were growing stronger and more organized with each victory. But Parliament was determined to demonstrate that it controlled the colonies. In 1773, the Tea Act was passed. This allowed British tea to be sold directly to colonial merchants less expensively than tea from other countries. Even though the British tea was cheaper to buy, the colonists resented this attempt to control the tea trade in America.

The colonists reacted swiftly. That December in Boston, a group of men dressed as Indians boarded a British ship and dumped its cargo of 343 boxes of tea into the harbor. The men were members of the Sons of Liberty, a group of Patriots, or people who were opposed to English rule. This act of defiance at Boston Harbor became known as the Boston Tea Party.

Crowds cheered as the Sons of Liberty returned to shore after dumping British tea into Boston Harbor in December 1773.

To punish the colonists for their defiance, Parliament closed Boston Harbor. No goods, including food, could enter Boston by ship. This caused may colonists to lose their jobs. Soon the citizens of Boston were going hungry.

Other colonies quickly took steps to support the Bostonians. When the House of Burgesses passed a resolution supporting the Massachusetts colonists, the governor disbanded the house. The members gathered instead at Raleigh Tavern in Williamsburg for a meeting called the First Virginia Convention. There, they made plans to invite representatives from all thirteen colonies to discuss what should be done about England. Delegates, or representatives, from Virginia were chosen during the First Virginia Convention.

The Continental Congress

September 5, 1774, marked the first meeting of representatives from all thirteen colonies. Calling themselves the Continental Congress, the representatives elected Peyton Randolph, a Virginian, as president. George Washington, Patrick Henry, and Richard Henry Lee were among the other delegates from Virginia.

After much discussion, the congress agreed to demand that Parliament treat the colonists the same as other British citizens. The colonists would thus be allowed to enact their own laws. Britain did not respond to the demands of the

Continental Congress, so the delegates agreed to meet again the following May. In the meantime, British troops and ships began making their way to America's shores.

On April 19, 1775, British troops marched into Lexington and Concord, Massachusetts. Patriot Paul Revere had ridden ahead to warn the minutemen. The minutemen were Patriot militiamen who got their name from their ability to be ready quickly to fight. They were waiting when the British arrived. The battles ended with the British retreating to Boston. The Revolutionary War had begun.

Dunmore's Proclamation

Following the Second Virginia Convention, many colonists joined militias to fight against the British. Governor John Murray (also known as Lord Dunmore) wanted to stop them. In November 1775, he made an official announcement. He declared martial law in Virginia. This meant the British army controlled Virginia's government. He also offered freedom to any slaves who would fight for England. This caused a great uproar in the colony. The governor thought this would make Virginians less likely to join militias. Instead, Dunmore's Proclamation pushed many undecided colonists to side with the Patriots. They believed that Dunmore was encouraging a slave revolt. In addition, giving slaves a reward for leaving their masters to fight threatened many farmers' ability to grow their crops and make money. The proclamation made many Virginians realize that they shared Patriot ideals.

The Second Continental Congress met in May. The delegates chose George Washington to serve as commander of the Continental army. This was a challenging job for Washington. The army was made up of volunteers and members of colonial militias rather than professional soldiers. There were no uniforms, little money with which to pay the soldiers, and limited weapons. Washington had to rely upon quick raids rather than large-scale attacks.

During the winter of 1777, it seemed that the Americans might have to give up. The soldiers were starving. Some had no shoes to wear in the snow, and their clothing was threadbare. They were running out of ammunition and weapons. That spring, however, France agreed to join with the colonists in their fight against England. With the troops and supplies provided by the French, the Continental army was able to launch major attacks on the British troops.

Declarations of Independence

In June 1776, the Virginia Convention declared Virginia's independence from England. A constitution (a written plan of government) was created for the new **Commonwealth** of Virginia. This document established legislative and executive branches for the state government. Members of the two houses of the legislature would elect a governor. The governor would be limited to serving only a certain number of years.

The Articles of Confederation

In 1777, the Continental Congress created the Articles of Confederation. This set of laws was the basis for the first national government for the United States. Under the Articles of Confederation, the individual states kept most of the power. They were like small nations, each with its own money, laws, and taxes. The Articles of Confederation helped the states work together during the Revolutionary War. When the war was over, however, the new nation discovered that the articles were not a strong enough system of laws. To replace them, the nation's leaders created a new set of laws called the Constitution.

The new constitution included the Virginia Declaration of Rights. This document, written by George Mason, outlined a Bill of Rights, which limited the government's power and protected the rights of ordinary citizens.

A month later, Thomas Jefferson drafted the Declaration of Independence for the United States. He used the Virginia declaration as a model. This document told the English king and the world that the thirteen colonies were no longer part of England. They were now the United States of America. The members of the Second Continental Congress agreed upon the final wording of the declaration on July 4, 1776. The following month, the delegates signed the document and made it official.

The Last Battle

After the battles at Lexington and Concord, American and British forces fought bitterly for more than six years. Few of the battles of the Revolutionary War took place in Virginia. But British troops marched through the state, looting and burning several towns and cities. In the summer of 1781, General Washington got word that General Charles Cornwallis was headed to Yorktown, Virginia, with his British troops. Knowing that the admiral of the French navy was due to arrive in Chesapeake Bay that fall, Washington slipped out of New York with his troops and marched south to Virginia.

The French fleet arrived in Chesapeake Bay at the beginning of September. When Washington arrived with his troops later that month, Cornwallis was surrounded. The British were fired upon from all sides both day and night. Finally, three weeks later, Cornwallis surrendered to Washington. The United States had won its independence from England.

CHAPTER EIGHT

The Commonwealth of Virginia

A New Nation

Although the British surrendered in 1781, negotiations for the peace treaty took two more years. Finally, in 1783, the United States was officially a new nation. Now, there was much discussion about whether the type of government described in the Articles of Confederation would be successful over time. Many of the nation's leaders, including George Washington, believed that the **federal government** needed more power. Other Americans were not convinced. They believed that a strong central government would interfere with individual and state rights.

The Constitutional Convention met in Philadelphia in 1787 to consider revisions to the Articles of Confederation.

General George Washington approved a new thirteen-star flag representing the new United States of America.

Virginians argued over whether to accept the Constitution. They finally agreed to ratify it after being assured that their individual rights would be protected.

The members soon came to the conclusion that they had to create a whole new set of laws for the new country. After much debate, the delegates wrote this new set of laws, called the Constitution.

The Constitution of the United States of America set up the government of the new country. It said that there would be three branches of government—the legislative, executive, and judicial branches. This was done so that no one branch of the government could become too powerful. The legislative body, Congress, would have two houses. The Senate would be made up of two representatives from each state. However, the number of members in the House of Representatives would be based on each state's population.

The delegates took the Constitution back to their states for approval. In order for it to become the official law of the land, two-thirds of the thirteen states had to approve it. By June 21, 1788, nine states had approved the Constitution, and it became the foundation of the U.S. government.

Even though Virginia contributed so many ideas and leaders to the Revolutionary War, it was not one of the first nine states to **ratify** the Constitution. The people living in the Tidewater and western regions agreed with the kind of government written about in the Constitution. However, Thomas Jefferson and others in the Piedmont area wanted stronger protection for individual rights, including freedom of religion. The states then agreed to include a Bill of Rights in the Constitution. These rights would be similar to those outlined in the Virginia Declaration of Rights. With this compromise, Virginia became the tenth state to join the United States, on June 25, 1788.

Virginia's Statute for Religious Freedom

Virginia had declared its independence from Britain in 1776. Many of its citizens played a leading role in the development of the United States. The influence of Virginia's citizens did not end with the Revolutionary War. It continued into the first decades of the new country's history.

In 1780, Virginia's capital moved from Williamsburg to Richmond. The state legislature met after the Revolutionary War ended. It tackled the issue of government-supported religion. From the colony's beginning, the Anglican Church had been supported by Virginia's royal government. The colonists paid taxes that were used to support the church. Leaders of the colony had often been judged fit for office based on their religious beliefs.

After the Revolutionary War, Virginians had to decide whether tax money should still be used to support religion. Some believed that churches should be supported by the state. They said that taxes could be paid to the church of one's choosing, rather than a single, official, state-approved church. Others, led by Thomas Jefferson and James Madison, believed that churches and the government should be completely separate. This group believed that taxes should never be used to support churches, even one's own church.

In 1786, Jefferson wrote the Statute for Religious Freedom. The statute (law) points out that "civil rights have no dependence on our religious opinions, more than our opinions in physics or geometry." It declares that people should have the freedom to worship, or not worship, as they please.

ALMIGHTY GOD HATH CREATED THE MIND FREE. ALL ATTEMPTS TO INFLUENCE IT BY TEMPORAL PUNISHMENTS OR BURTHENS···ARE A DEPARTURE FROM THE PLAN OF THE HOLY AUTHOR OF OUR RELIGION···NO MAN SHALL BE COMPELLED TO FREQUENT OR SUPPORT ANY RELIGIOUS WORSHIP OR MINISTRY OR SHALL OTHERWISE SUFFER ON ACCOUNT OF HIS RELIGIOUS OPINIONS OR BELIEF, BUT ALL MEN SHALL BE FREE TO PROFESS AND BY ARGUMENT TO MAINTAIN, THEIR OPINIONS IN MATTERS OF RELIGION. I KNOW BUT ONE CODE OF MORALITY FOR MEN WHETHER ACTING SINGLY OR COLLECTIVELY.

This passage from the Virginia Statute for Religious Freedom is written in stone at the Jefferson Memorial in Washington, DC.

Jefferson wrote the Declaration of Independence and served as a U.S. president. But he considered the passage of the Statute for Religious Freedom his finest achievement.

Mother of Eight Presidents

The leadership role that Virginia took before and during the Revolutionary War continued as the United States began to grow. George Washington enjoyed tremendous popularity after the British surrender at Yorktown. Many Americans were willing to crown him king. He refused this honor.

In 1789, Washington was elected America's first president. He faced the challenge of protecting the new Constitution while at the same time molding the thirteen states into one strong nation. He was especially careful not to use his influence to expand the power of the executive branch of the government beyond what the Constitution had established. This set an important example for future presidents who might have been tempted to override the independence of Congress or the courts.

After serving two terms, Washington retired. It was time for a peaceful, constitutional transfer of power to a new president. After John Adams's inauguration as president in 1797, Washington returned to Mount Vernon, his home in Virginia. Two years later, he died from a sudden illness.

Virginia's most famous citizen, George Washington, took the oath of office and became the first president of the United States of America on April 30, 1789.

In tribute to George Washington, Adams said, "His example is now complete, and it will teach wisdom and **virtue** to magistrates, citizens, and men, not only in the present age but in future generations as long as our history shall be read."

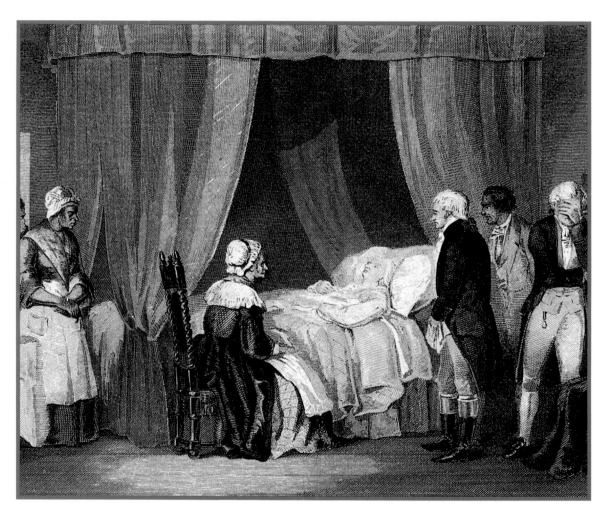

President Washington died at his farm at Mount Vernon only two years after leaving office.

George Washington was not the only Virginian to lead the United States. Four of the first five presidents—George Washington, Thomas Jefferson, James Madison, and James Monroe—were born in Virginia. Four other Virginians—William Henry Harrison, John Tyler, Zachary Taylor, and Woodrow Wilson—were later elected president of the United States. Because of this record, Virginia gained a reputation as "the Mother of Presidents."

Notable Virginians

- George Washington, commander of the Continental army and first president of the United States
- Thomas Jefferson, author of the Declaration of Independence and third president
- James Madison, primary author of the Constitution and fourth president
- James Monroe, fifth president

- Patrick Henry, delegate to the Continental Congress and first governor of the Commonwealth of Virginia
- John Marshall, third chief justice of the Supreme Court
- William Henry Harrison, ninth president
- John Tyler, tenth president
- Zachary Taylor, twelfth president
- Woodrow Wilson, twenty-eighth president

Recipe
Corn Pone

Corn was an important part of the Algonquian Indians' diet. These natives shared their methods of planting and cooking with the early colonists. One of the dishes they made was pone, a baked corn cake. This recipe for corn pone is adapted for modern kitchens but will give you a taste of a food that has been made in Virginia for centuries.

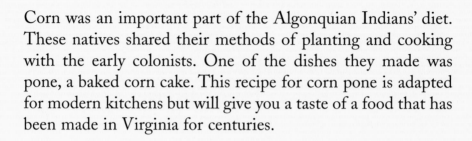

Bacon fat or vegetable oil for pan
3 cups white cornmeal
1 teaspoon salt
3 tablespoons melted bacon fat
or vegetable oil
5 cups boiling water

- Preheat oven to 400°F.
- Grease a shallow baking sheet with bacon fat or vegetable oil.
- Put the cornmeal in a bowl, and add the salt and fat.
- Add boiling water until the dough is the consistency of thick batter.
- Drop from a spoon onto the prepared baking sheet in stick or oval shapes.
- Bake for 40 minutes.
- Serve hot.

This activity should be done with adult supervision.

Activity
Making a Quilt

The quilting bee was a popular activity for colonial women, who socialized while sewing fabric scraps together to create unique bedcovers called quilts. These beautiful quilts were a necessity to keep the family warm on cold winter nights.

You can make a quilt using cut paper.

Procedure

Butcher paper • Ruler or yardstick • Heavy construction paper or card stock • Scissors • Tape • Markers and crayons • Glue or paste

- Using the construction paper or card stock, create a pattern for a quilt piece. Use triangles, squares, and rectangles to form any object you like—a tree, a snowflake, a house.
- Cut a piece of butcher paper to the full size of your quilt. Tape two pieces together, if desired, for a larger quilt.
- Trace the card stock quilt pattern onto the butcher paper. Repeat until the butcher paper is covered with the pattern. Count the number of times that the traced pattern is repeated.

- Create the same number of paper quilt pieces by tracing the pattern on construction paper or card stock.
- Decorate each quilt piece. You can:
  - cut out geometric shapes that combine to create everyday objects and paste them on the quilt piece.
  - cut out random shapes and paste them on the quilt piece.
  - color each quilt piece.
- Paste or glue each quilt piece onto one of the traced outlines on the butcher paper.
- Display and enjoy!

This activity should be done with adult supervision.

VIRGINIA
Time Line

1585
The first English colonists settle on Roanoke Island.

1607
Jamestown becomes the first permanent English settlement in America.

1619
The House of Burgesses is established.

1639
King Charles reestablishes the House of Burgesses.

1575   1600   1625   1650   1675

1590
John White returns to Roanoke Colony and finds it has been abandoned.

1614
Tobacco is introduced in Virginia.

1624
King James declares Virginia a royal colony and disbands the House of Burgesses.

1676
Bacon's Rebellion.

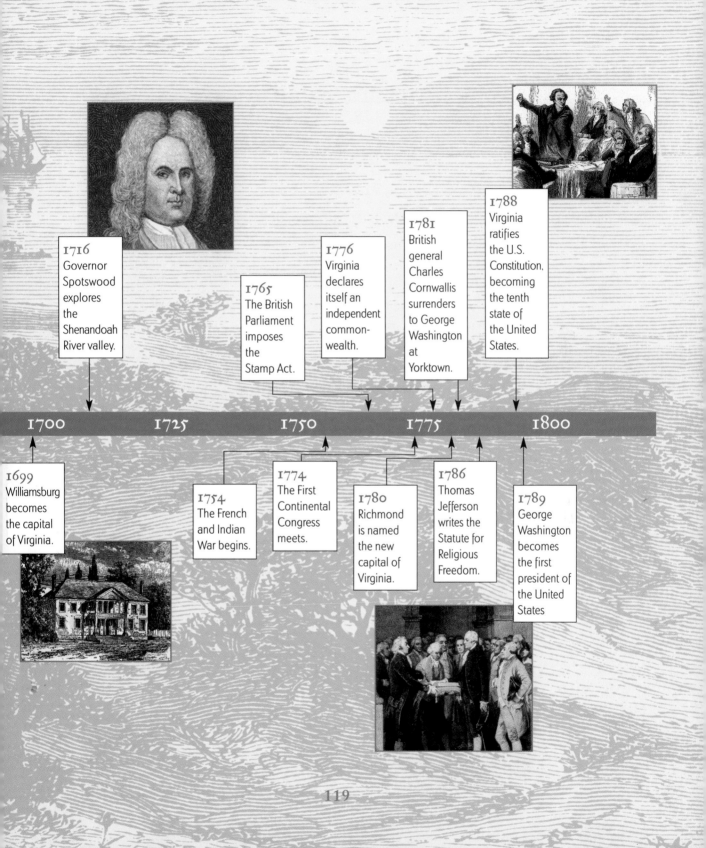

1716
Governor Spotswood explores the Shenandoah River valley.

1765
The British Parliament imposes the Stamp Act.

1776
Virginia declares itself an independent common-wealth.

1781
British general Charles Cornwallis surrenders to George Washington at Yorktown.

1788
Virginia ratifies the U.S. Constitution, becoming the tenth state of the United States.

1700   1725   1750   1775   1800

1699
Williamsburg becomes the capital of Virginia.

1754
The French and Indian War begins.

1774
The First Continental Congress meets.

1780
Richmond is named the new capital of Virginia.

1786
Thomas Jefferson writes the Statute for Religious Freedom.

1789
George Washington becomes the first president of the United States

119

Further Reading

Cocke, William. *A Historical Album of Virginia.* Brookfield, CT: Millbrook Press, 1995.

Collier, Christopher, and James Lincoln Collier. *The Paradox of Jamestown.* New York, NY: Benchmark Books, 1998.

Hakim, Joy. *A History of Us: Making Thirteen Colonies.* New York, NY: Oxford University Press, 1993.

Harriot, Thomas. *A Briefe and True Report of the New Found Land of Virginia.* New York, NY: Dover, 1972.

Masoff, Joy. *Colonial Times 1600–1700.* New York, NY: Scholastic Reference, 2000.

McDaniel, Melissa. *The Powhatan Indians.* New York, NY: Chelsea House, 1996.

Glossary

archaeologist a scientist who studies past human
  civilizations

charter a contract that gives the holder the right to settle
  land in the king's name

commonwealth a state founded on law and united for the
  common good of the people

delegate a person who represents the views of a group of
  people

expedition a journey for exploration

federal government a central government that shares
  power with member territories of the federation

grant a legal document giving someone ownership of a
  piece of land

immigrant someone who travels to a country to settle and
  make a new home

indentured servant a person who agrees to work for a
  specific number of years in exchange for travel expenses

knight a high-ranking soldier

massacre the murder of a large number of people

missionary person who attempts to change the religious beliefs of others to match his or her own

mutiny rebellion against one in authority

palisade a fence of pointed stakes that is built for protection

peninsula land surrounded on three sides by water

ratify to approve by a formal agreement

resolution formal decision or conclusion reached after a meeting, often after a vote

tenant farmer one who rents farmland and pays with either cash or crops

tribute gifts of food or other goods given to a leader

vengeance use of extreme action to get revenge

virtue goodness or moral excellence

Index